T2-BPL-393

D0820111

MATH ADVENTURES

Treasure Hunt in the Jungle

by Wendy Clemson
and David Clemson

Math and curriculum
consultant: Debra Voege, M.A.,
science and math curriculum
resource teacher

GARETH**STEVENS**
GS
PUBLISHING
A Member of the WRC Media Family of Companies

Please visit our web site at: www.garethstevens.com
For a free color catalog describing Gareth Stevens Publishing's
list of high-quality books and multimedia programs,
call 1-800-542-2595 (USA) or 1-800-387-3178 (Canada).
Gareth Stevens Publishing's fax: (414) 332-3567

Library of Congress Cataloging-in-Publication Data

Clemson, Wendy.
 Treasure hunt in the jungle / Wendy Clemson and David
Clemson. — North American ed.
    p. cm. — (Math adventures)
 ISBN-13: 978-0-8368-7842-4 (lib. bdg.)
 ISBN-13: 978-0-8368-8141-7 (softcover)
 1. Mathematics—Problems, exercises, etc.—Juvenile literature. 2. Treasure Island
(Imaginary place)—Juvenile literature. I. Clemson, David. II. Title.
QA43.C657   2006
510—dc22
                                                    2006052244

This North American edition first published in 2007 by
Gareth Stevens Publishing
A Member of the WRC Media Family of Companies
330 West Olive Street, Suite 100
Milwaukee, WI 53212 USA

This U.S. edition copyright © 2007 by Gareth Stevens, Inc.
Original edition copyright © 2007 by ticktock Entertainment Ltd.
First published in Great Britain in 2006 by ticktock Media Ltd., Unit 2,
Orchard Business Centre, North Farm Road, Tunbridge Wells, Kent, TN2 3XF.

ticktock project editor: Rebecca Clunes
ticktock project designer: Sara Greasley
Gareth Stevens editor: Tea Benduhn
Gareth Stevens art direction: Tammy West
Gareth Stevens graphic designer: Kami Strunsee
Gareth Stevens production: Jessica Yanke and Robert Kraus

Picture credits
t=top, b=bottom, c=center, l=left, r=right
Amazon-Images/Alamy 2, 19t; Yann Arthus-Bertrand/Corbis 29; e.t. archive 1; Wolfgang Kaehler/Alamy 11;
Shutterstock 4tl, 4tr, 4bl, 4br, 5, 7, 8, 9, 10, 13, 14, 15, 16b, 16c, 16t, 17b, 17t, 18, 19b, 20, 21, 22, 23,
24-25, 27, 30, 31b, 31t, 32; ticktock Media image archive 6l; Werner Forman Archive 6r.

Printed in Canada

1 2 3 4 5 6 7 8 9 10 10 09 08 07 06

CONTENTS

MEASUREMENT CONVERSIONS

1 inch = 2.5 centimeters   1 mile = 1.6 kilometers
1 foot = 0.3 meter   1 pound = 0.5 kilogram
1 yard = 1 meter

BE AN EXPLORER

You are an explorer. Explorers find amazing places that very few people have ever seen. You travel all over the world. Today, you are going on an adventure to search for hidden treasure. If you find any treasure, you will give it to a museum so everyone can see it!

Exploring the world is an exciting and important job!

Explorers climb mountains and trek through jungles.

Sometimes, explorers see wild and unusual animals!

Explorers find treasures and ancient ruins that tell us about the past.

Explorers sometimes have to camp in very cold or very hot places.

Did you know that explorers need to use math?

Inside this book, you will find math puzzles that explorers have to solve every day. You will also have a chance to answer number questions about the things you find as you explore.

What is inside the book?

Find out what needs to be done in your busy day.

Charts and tables will help you answer the math questions.

Fact boxes tell you more about the places you explore.

Answer the questions and practice your math skills.

If you get stuck, there are some tips to help you on pages 30 and 31.

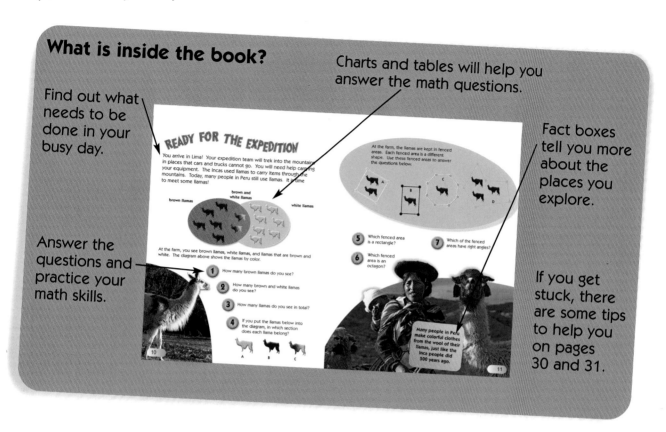

Are you ready to be an explorer for the day?

You will need paper, a pencil, and a ruler, and don't forget to bring your backpack. Let's go!

LOOKING FOR TREASURE

You are going on a trip to Peru, which is a country in South America. On your adventure, you will climb mountains and explore the thick, dark rain forest. You will see ruins and unusual animals. If you are lucky, you might find Incan treasure to give to a museum in Peru!

The Incas lived in Peru about 500 years ago. The picture to the left is an Incan painting of 10 warriors.

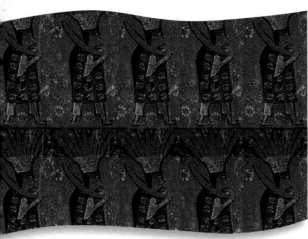

Incan kings counted their people in groups of 10, 100, and 1,000. The groups made it easier for the kings to know how many people they ruled in total.

The Incas used gold and silver to make lots of things, such as the gold mask above.

1 How many groups of 10 are in 40?

2 How many groups of 10 are in 110?

3 If you put 82 people in groups of 10, how many groups of 10 will there be? How many people will be left over?

4 Round each of these numbers to the nearest 10.
A 33   B 65   C 78
D 40   E 96

5 Which of the following numbers have a 5 in the hundreds place?
35   579   56
1,509   1,536

Machu Picchu was built in about 1440. It was a sacred place high in the Andes Mountains.

OFF TO PERU!

You are part of a team of explorers. The members of your team are coming from all over the world. You will meet your team members in Lima, which is the capital city of Peru. Many of the explorers in the team have long airplane flights to reach Peru.

FLIGHT TIMES TO LIMA

leaving from	going to	flight time
London, England	Lima, Peru	17 hours
Washington, D.C., United States	Lima, Peru	11 hours
Moscow, Russia	Lima, Peru	21 hours
Mexico City, Mexico	Lima, Peru	6 hours
Nairobi, Kenya (Africa)	Lima, Peru	29 hours

1 Look at the flight times chart above. How long will it take to get from Washington, D.C., to Lima?

2 How long will it take to get from Moscow to Lima?

3 Which flight will take the least time?

4 Which flight will take longer than 1 day?

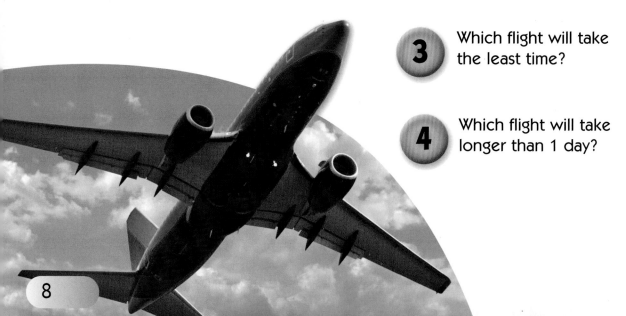

To get to Lima, you must fly over the Andes Mountains. The Andes form the longest mountain range in the world. They cover 5,500 miles!

Use the flight times chart to answer the questions on this page.

5 If you leave Washington, D.C., at 12:00, which clock below shows your arrival time in Lima?

A

B

C

6 If an explorer leaves Mexico City at 3:00, which clock shows her or his arrival time in Lima?

A

B

C

READY FOR THE EXPEDITION

You arrive in Lima! Your expedition team will trek into the mountains to places that cars and trucks cannot go. You will need help carrying your equipment. The Incas used llamas to carry items through the mountains. Today, many people in Peru still use llamas. It is time to meet some llamas!

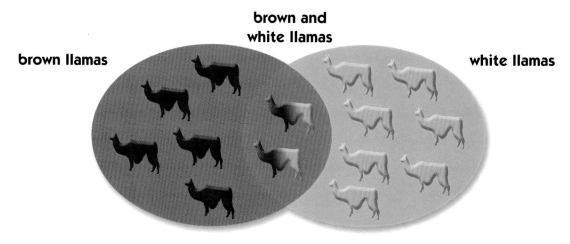

brown and white llamas

brown llamas

white llamas

At a llama farm, you see brown llamas, white llamas, and llamas that are brown and white. The diagram above shows the llamas by color.

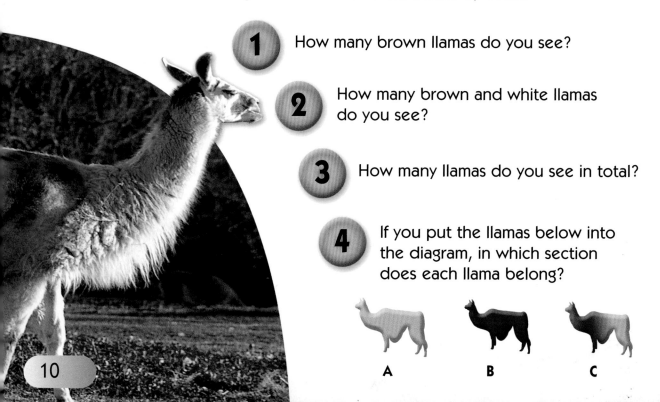

1 How many brown llamas do you see?

2 How many brown and white llamas do you see?

3 How many llamas do you see in total?

4 If you put the llamas below into the diagram, in which section does each llama belong?

A   B   C

At the farm, the llamas are kept in fenced areas. Each fenced area is a different shape. Use these fenced areas to answer the questions below.

A

B

C

D

5 Which fenced area is a rectangle?

6 Which fenced area is an octagon?

7 Which of the fenced areas have right angles?

Many people in Peru make colorful clothes from the wool of llamas, just like the Incas did 500 years ago.

THE TREASURE MAP

You go with your team to look for an Incan temple hidden deep in the jungle. No other explorer has been able to find the temple, but you have an old map that shows you where the temple might be! You will begin your journey in the mountains, using stony roads that the Incas built.

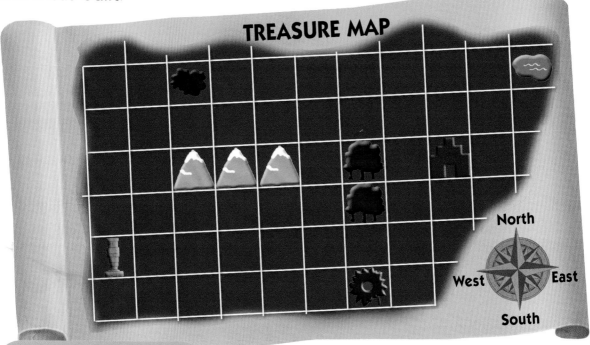

TREASURE MAP

North
West — East
South

MAP KEY

 = pool

 = swamp

 = mountains

 = rare flowers

 = temple

 = jungle

 = statue

Look at the treasure map. Are the following statements true or false?

 1 The jungle is north of the rare flowers.

 2 The mountains are east of the temple.

 3 The pool is east of the swamp.

Look at the treasure map again. Where will you end up if you follow the directions below?

4 Start at the statue. Go 2 squares right and 2 squares up.

5 Start at the swamp. Go 4 squares right and 2 squares down.

6 Start at the pool. Go 1 square down, 2 squares left, and 1 square down.

7 The Incas built good roads. To measure the width of an Incan road, would you use feet or miles?

8 To measure the length of an Incan road, would you use feet or miles?

The Incas built roads to help people travel around Peru. Some roads went from one end of their kingdom to the other.

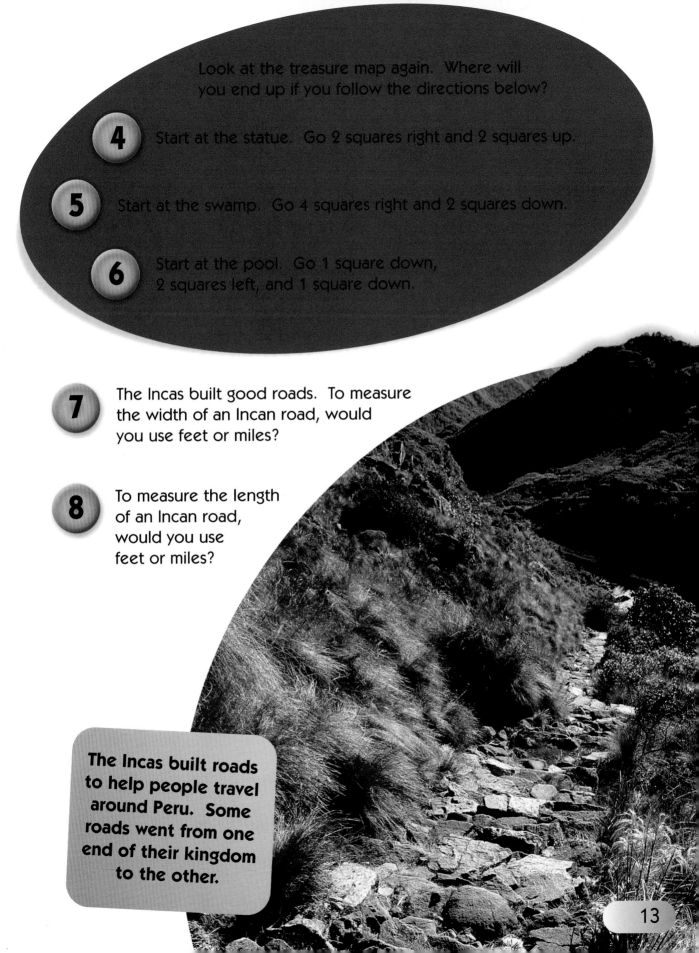

HIGH IN THE MOUNTAINS

Being an explorer can be very difficult! You often trek along steep, rocky roads through the mountains. When you are high in the mountains, the air is thin. The thin air makes it hard to breathe. Thankfully, you planned your trip for May, when the weather in Peru is not too hot or too cold.

MONTHS OF THE YEAR

1 Look at the months of the year to the right. Put them in the correct order.

2 If the expedition lasts through the end of May, what month will it be when you go home?

May	April	September
June	August	January
July	October	November
February	December	March

WOW! You just saw a condor. The condor is one of the biggest birds in the world. These giant birds live high in the Andes Mountains.

Condors don't flap their giant wings very often. Instead, they keep their wings spread out to glide through the air.

From tip to tip, a condor's wings measure 9½ feet across.

3 How many inches are in 1 foot?

4 How many inches are in ½ foot?

5 How many feet are in 1 yard?

6 Is 9½ feet longer or shorter than 3 yards?

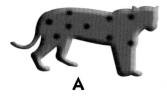

INTO THE JUNGLE

You are following the treasure map into the jungle. Explorers take photographs of and make notes about everything they see on an expedition. The jungle is full of wild and unusual animals. You hear a roar. What made that noise? It is a very big, wild cat called a jaguar.

Jaguars are covered with spots. A jaguar's spots help it hide from other animals when it is hunting. Look at the jaguars below to answer the following questions.

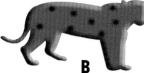

A

B

C

1 Which of the jaguars above has an odd number of spots?

2 Which jaguar has the most spots?

3 Which jaguar has the fewest spots?

4 Which jaguars have even numbers of spots?

5 Everywhere you look in the jungle, you see little squirrel monkeys. How many squirrel monkeys do you see on these pages?

Squirrel monkeys live in groups called troops. There are normally 40 to 50 monkeys in one troop. Sometimes, there can be as many as 200!

6 Try these monkey puzzles!

A 2 monkeys + 2 monkeys + 2 monkeys = ?
B 3 x 2 monkeys = ?
C 2 monkeys + 6 monkeys = ?
D 4 monkeys – 2 monkeys = ?
E 2 x 2 monkeys = ?

ON THE JUNGLE FLOOR

On the ground, you see thousands of tiny insects and jungle creatures. Some of the creatures you see are leaf-cutter ants! They are collecting pieces of leaves and are taking them back to their nest. The ants use the leaves for food.

A leaf-cutter ant can carry a piece of leaf that weighs 20 times its own body weight.

1 Look at the group of leaf-cutter ants in the box below. How many ants do you think are in the box? Try to say how many without counting them. Now, count them. How many ants are in the box?

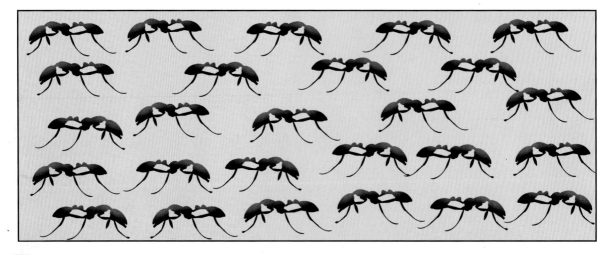

2 What is the number of ants in the box rounded to the nearest ten?

You see a tiny poison dart frog. This kind of frog has deadly, poisonous skin that stops snakes and big spiders from eating them!

Some poison dart frogs are only 1/2 inch long.

Poison dart frogs come in lots of different colors. Add the frogs below.

3 🐸🐸🐸🐸 + 🐸🐸 = **?**

4 🐸🐸🐸 + 🐸🐸🐸🐸🐸🐸 = **?**

5 🐸🐸🐸🐸🐸🐸 + 🐸🐸🐸 + 🐸🐸🐸 = **?**

6 Millipedes live in the jungle, too. "Millipede" means 1,000 feet, but most millipedes only have between 80 and 400 feet. Which of the numbers below are between 80 and 400?

66	81
42	300
93	88
410	100

JUNGLE BUTTERFLIES AND BIRDS

You have been trekking through the jungle for 5 days! You walk about 10 miles each day. Your explorer's notebook is filling up with notes about exciting jungle animals.

EXPLORER'S NOTEBOOK

jungle animals	number seen
jaguars	3
blue poison dart frogs	10
millipedes	9
blue morpho butterflies	16
red poison dart frogs	22

1 Look at the explorer's notebook to the left. How many millipedes have you seen?

2 Which animal have you seen 16 of?

3 How many poison dart frogs have you seen in total?

4 The butterfly above is a blue morpho butterfly. It lives in the jungles of South America. Use your ruler to measure across the butterfly's wings. How wide is the butterfly's wingspan?

Toucans are not very good at flying. They hop from tree branch to tree branch!

5 You see a toucan up in a tree. Its orange beak is 8 inches long. Its body is 25 inches long. Complete these math puzzles, which use 25 and 8.

A
25 + 25

B
25 + 8

C
25 − 8

D
8 + 8

DISCOVERING THE TEMPLE

Suddenly, through the thick trees and bushes, you spot the ruins of a building. The map was right! You have found an Incan temple. The Incas built lots of temples for their many different gods. The temple you have found is one the Incas built for their Sun god.

The Incas did not use anything like cement to hold stones together. They chose stones that were shaped to fit together well.

1 If the shapes below were stones, which one would be the best to use for building?

 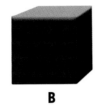  

A   B   C   D

2 Match these names to the shapes above.

cylinder   **cube**   **sphere**   **pyramid**

The bricks below are being used to build a large triangle shape. They are the bottom two rows of the shape.

3 How many bricks should be in the next row up?

4 How many bricks should be in the row above that?

5 How many bricks should be at the top of the triangle?

6 Now try a different brick pattern. A wall has 30 bricks, then 25 bricks, then 20 bricks. How many bricks are in the next row?

23

INSIDE THE TEMPLE

Your expedition team splits up into 4 groups to explore the temple. Long ago, the Incan kings split, or divided, their kingdom into 4 equal parts. Their word for the kingdom was "Tawantinsuyu," which means "Land of the four quarters."

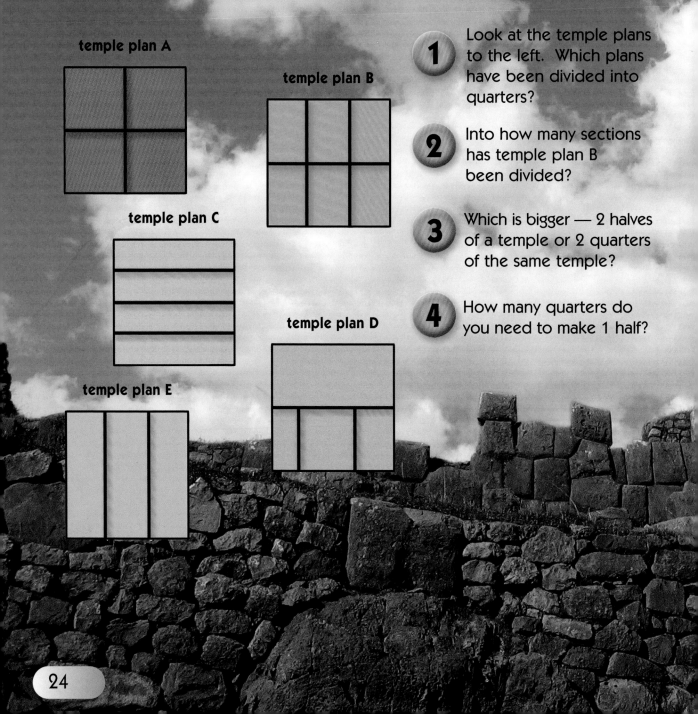

temple plan A

temple plan B

temple plan C

temple plan D

temple plan E

1 Look at the temple plans to the left. Which plans have been divided into quarters?

2 Into how many sections has temple plan B been divided?

3 Which is bigger — 2 halves of a temple or 2 quarters of the same temple?

4 How many quarters do you need to make 1 half?

The walls of the temple do not have any writing on them. The Incas did not have a written language. Instead of writing, they tied knots in pieces of string. Different numbers of knots had different meanings.

Look at these knot patterns. How many knots come next on each string?

5

6

7

TEMPLE TREASURES

The temple has many wonderful treasures inside. The Incan kings were very wealthy. Their people dug gold and silver out of the ground and made beautiful items with these precious metals. The Incas also used copper, bronze, stone, pottery, and wood to make items such as jewelry, statues, and drinking and cooking pots.

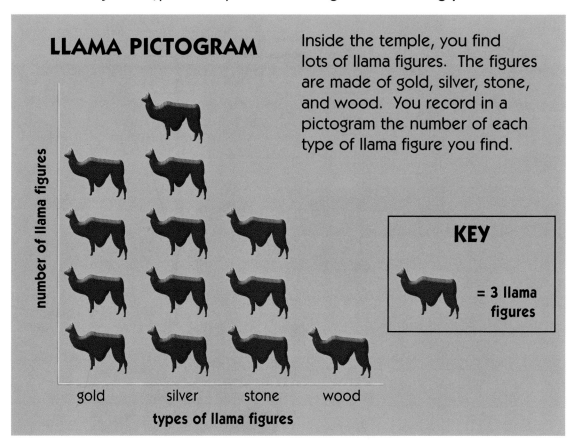

LLAMA PICTOGRAM

Inside the temple, you find lots of llama figures. The figures are made of gold, silver, stone, and wood. You record in a pictogram the number of each type of llama figure you find.

number of llama figures

gold   silver   stone   wood

types of llama figures

KEY

= 3 llama figures

Use the pictogram above to answer these questions.

1 How many gold llama figures did you find?

2 How many more silver llamas did you find than gold llamas?

3 How many more gold llamas did you find than wood llamas?

4 How many llama figures did you find in total?

While your team explores the temple, the llamas you brought rest among the ruins. They will have lots of exciting things to carry back to Lima.

Inti was the name of the Incan Sun god. The Incan Moon god was called Quilla. You find lots of Sun and Moon figures in the temple. Count them.

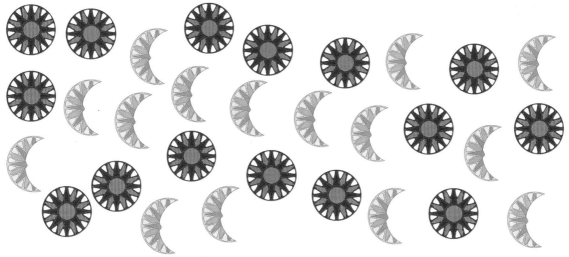

5 You need to pack the Suns and Moons into boxes of 10. How many boxes of 10 can you make?

6 The Sun and Moon figures each weigh 3 pounds. If a llama can carry 30 pounds on its back, how many llamas do you need to carry the Sun and Moon figures?

PATTERNS AND PICTURES

The Incas decorated items with patterns of squares and right angles. On the way home from your expedition, you will fly over some giant patterns called the Nazca lines. The Nazca lines are even older than the Inca civilization. They were made in the desert sand by people who lived in Peru 2,000 years ago!

1 The Incas often used a checkerboard pattern much like the one to the left. If you continued numbering the boxes as they appear here, what numbers would you find in the bottom row of the checkerboard?

2 Would the numbers below be on red or yellow squares?

   8   11
       17   20

3 Even numbers all fall on the same color squares. Are the squares red or yellow?

4 The patterns below are styles of an Incan pattern called a "tocapus." Trace each pattern with your finger. How many right angles does each pattern have?

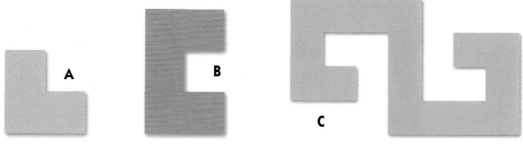

A

B

C

The Nazca drawings include animals, insects, birds, and patterns. As your plane flies over a giant spider drawing, you see it from different directions.

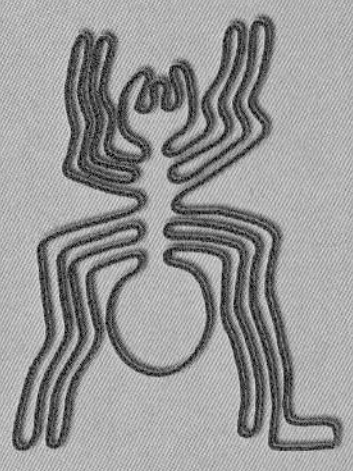

Look at the spider to the left. Your plane is flying clockwise.

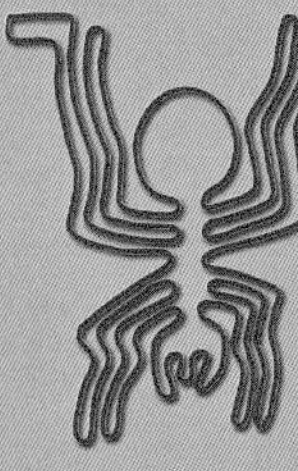

A

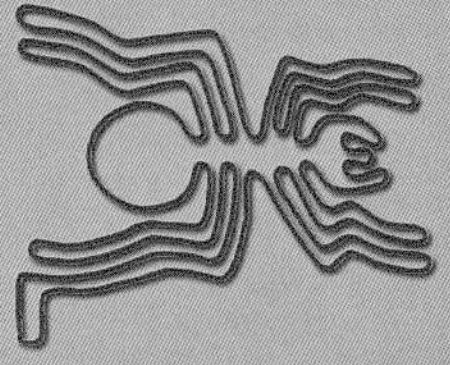

B

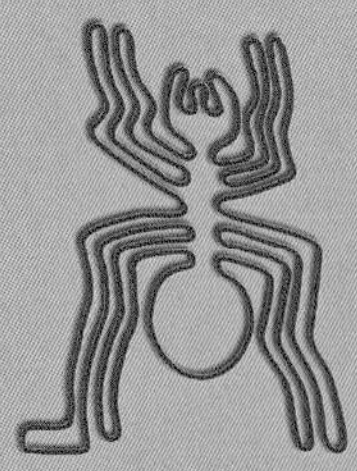

C

5 Which picture shows the spider after a quarter turn?

6 Which picture shows the spider after a flip?

This Nazca spider is 150 feet long! It is just one of the amazing things you have seen on your expedition in Peru.

TIPS AND HELP

PAGES 6-7

Rounding - To round a number to the nearest ten, make a number ending in 5, 6, 7, 8, or 9 bigger and make a number ending in 1, 2, 3, or 4 smaller. For example, 33 rounded to the nearest ten is 30, and 65 rounded to the nearest ten is 70.

Place value - We use only ten symbols to write all numbers. The place of each symbol gives its value. For example, 579 has a 5 in the hundreds place, a 7 in the tens place, and a 9 in the ones (or units) place, so we read this number as five hundred seventy-nine.

PAGES 8-9

Telling time - The shorter hand on a clock is the hour hand. It shows us what hour (or "o'clock") it is. The longer hand is the minute hand. It shows how many minutes until the hour or past the hour.

Hours in a day - There are 24 hours in 1 day.

PAGES 10-11

Sorting - The diagram is called a Venn diagram. It shows a set of brown llamas and a set of white llamas. The sets overlap so that the llamas that are both brown and white are in the brown set and in the white set.

Flat shapes - In math, a flat shape is said to have sides. Counting the sides is necessary to name flat shapes. A rectangle has 4 sides (with opposite sides that match in length) and 4 right angles. A square has 4 sides of equal length and 4 right angles. A hexagon has 6 sides. An octagon has 8 sides.

PAGES 12-13

Compass points - N, E, S, and W (north, east, south, and west) are the points of a compass. A compass can help us find our way. We can also use a compass to talk about directions.

PAGES 14-15

Months - There are 12 months in 1 year.

Measuring length - There are 12 inches in 1 foot. There are 3 feet in 1 yard.

PAGES 16-17

Odds and evens - Even numbers are in the pattern of counting by twos: 2, 4, 6, 8, and so on. Odd numbers are all the numbers that are not even: 1, 3, 5, 7, 9, and so on.

Calculation signs - These signs are used to do math calculations:
+ means add, plus, or sum
− means take away, minus, or subtract
x means multiply by or times
÷ means divide by or share by

PAGES 18-19

Estimating - To estimate an amount, look at all the information you have and decide what the answer might be.

Numbers between - Look at the hundreds, tens, and ones (or units). Any number that has at least 8 tens and 1 one, but not more than 3 hundreds, 9 tens, and 9 ones, is between 80 and 400.

PAGES 20-21

Measuring with a ruler - Make sure the "0" (zero) on the ruler is exactly at one end of the line you are measuring. Then read the number on the ruler at the other end of the line to find the width of the butterfly's wingspan.

PAGES 22-23

Solid shapes - A sphere is a perfectly round ball. A cube has 6 square faces and 8 corners. A pyramid has a square base, 4 sides that are triangles, and it comes to a point at the top. A cylinder has 2 faces that are circles, with 1 face at each end.

PAGES 24-25

Fractions - A fraction is part of a whole. When we cut or divide something into 4 equal parts, each part is the fraction ¼ (one quarter). If we cut something into 2 equal parts, each part is the fraction ½ (one-half).

Predicting patterns - Figuring out how a pattern will continue is called predicting, or imagining what will happen next. Count the knots and look for a pattern. Then, imagine that the same pattern continues across the page.

PAGES 26-27

Pictogram - In this kind of chart, a picture is used as a symbol for information. In this pictogram, 1 llama shape means 3 llama figures.

PAGES 28-29

Right angle - There are 4 right angles in 1 complete turn. A right angle is often shown like this:

right angle

A quarter turn - There are 4 quarter turns in 1 complete turn. Each quarter turn is a turn through a right angle.

Flip - a flip is a mirror image of the original image.

ANSWERS

PAGES 6-7

1. 4 groups
2. 11 groups
3. 8 groups, 2 people left over
4. A = 30   B = 70
   C = 80   D = 40
   E = 100
5. 579, 1,509, and 1,536

PAGES 8-9

1. 11 hours
2. 21 hours
3. Mexico City to Lima
4. Nairobi, Kenya to Lima
5. clock C
6. clock A

PAGES 10-11

1. 5 brown llamas
2. 2 brown and white llamas
3. 14 llamas
4. A = white llamas
   B = brown llamas
   C = brown and white llamas
5. B
6. C
7. A and B

PAGES 12-13

1. true
2. false
3. true
4. mountains
5. jungle
6. temple
7. feet
8. miles

PAGES 14-15

1. January, February, March, April, May, June, July, August, September, October, November, December
2. June
3. 12 inches
4. 6 inches
5. 3 feet
6. longer than 3 yards

PAGES 16-17

1. A
2. C
3. B
4. B and C
5. 8 squirrel monkeys
6. A = 6 monkeys
   B = 6 monkeys
   C = 8 monkeys
   D = 2 monkeys
   E = 4 monkeys

PAGES 18-19

1. 26 ants are in the box
2. 30 ants
3. 7 frogs
4. 9 frogs
5. 13 frogs
6. 81, 88, 93, 100, and 300

PAGES 20-21

1. 9 millipedes
2. blue morpho butterflies
3. 32 poison dart frogs
4. 4 inches wide
5. A = 50
   B = 33
   C = 17
   D = 16

PAGES 22-23

1. B
2. A = sphere
   B = cube
   C = pyramid
   D = cylinder
3. 3 bricks
4. 2 bricks
5. 1 brick
6. 15 bricks

PAGES 24-25

1. temple plan A and temple plan C
2. 6 sections
3. 2 halves
4. 2 quarters
5. 1 knot
6. 2 knots
7. 8 knots

PAGES 26-27

1. 12 gold llamas
2. 3 more silver llamas
3. 9 more gold llamas
4. 39 llama figures
5. 3 boxes of 10
6. 3 llamas

PAGES 28-29

1. 21, 22, 23, 24, and 25
2. 8 = yellow square
   11 = red square
   17 = red square
   20 = yellow square
3. yellow
4. A = 1 right angle
   B = 2 right angles
   C = 6 right angles
5. B
6. C